PETS' GUIDES

Squeak's Guide to

Caring Your Rats Mice

Isabel Thomas

raintree
a Capstone company — publishers for children

Raintree is an imprint of Capstone Global Library Limited, a company incorporated in England and Wales having its registered office at 7 Pilgrim Street, London, EC4V 6LB – Registered company number: 6695582

www.raintreepublishers.co.uk
myorders@raintreepublishers.co.uk

Text © Capstone Global Library Limited 2015
First published in hardback in 2014
Paperback edition first published in 2015
The moral rights of the proprietor have been asserted.

Edited by James Benefield and Brynn Baker
Designed by Cynthia Akiyoshi
Picture research by Tracy Cummins
Production by Victoria Fitzgerald
Originated by Capstone Global Library Limited
Printed and bound in China by RR Donnelley Asia

ISBN 978-1-406-28180-4 (hardback)
18 17 16 15 14
10 9 8 7 6 5 4 3 2 1
ISBN 978-1-406-28187-3 (paperback)
19 18 17 16 15
10 9 8 7 6 5 4 3 2 1

British Library Cataloguing in Publication Data
A full catalogue record for this book is available from the British Library.

Acknowledgements
We would like to thank the following for permission to reproduce photographs:

Alamy: © blickwinkel, 21, © Juniors Bildarchiv GmbH, 12, 17, 18, 27; Capstone Library: Karon Dubke, 10, 23, 25; Getty Images: Chris Scuffins, 7, Ron Levine, 5, 9; Glow Images: ARCO / Schulte, front cover; Superstock: Big Cheese Photo, 15; Design ElementsShutterstock: iBird, Picsfive, R-studio.

We would like to thank Eric Jukes for his assistance in the preparation of this book.

Every effort has been made to contact copyright holders of material reproduced in this book. Any omissions will be rectified in subsequent printings if notice is given to the publisher.

All the Internet addresses (URLs) given in this book were valid at the time of going to press. However, due to the dynamic nature of the Internet, some addresses may have changed, or sites may have changed or ceased to exist since publication. While the author and publisher regret any inconvenience this may cause readers, no responsibility for any such changes can be accepted by either the author or the publisher.

Contents

Some words are shown in bold, **like this**. You can find out what they mean by looking in the glossary.

Do you want pet rats or mice?

Hello! I'm Squeak and this book is all about pets like me. Rats and mice are **rodents**, and we make great pets. It's fun to watch us play and explore. You can teach us to snuggle in your hands, and even sit on your shoulder.

Before getting pet rats or mice, be sure you can look after us properly. We'll need food, water and a clean place to live. Plus, we need company, safe toys to play with and **vet** care if we get sick or injured. In return, we'll be your best friends.

Choosing your rats or mice

It's time to meet some more mice and rats. Check out our different **coats** and colours. Rats and mice have similar needs but are slightly different animals. For example, rats are bigger than mice. They need larger homes and more food.

In the wild, rats and mice live in groups. If possible, I like to have company, especially when I am asleep. If you would like to keep a rat or a mouse, think about buying a friend for me if you can.

Mice or rats are a good choice if you have no other pets. We're afraid of animals such as cats and dogs. Never keep mice with rats or other types of rodents. We need company of our own kind.

Animal shelters, **rescue centres**, **breeders**, and pet shops are the best places to find us. Ask the on-site expert to help you choose mice or rats that know each other. For example, girl mice make good pets, but boy mice may fight each other. Boy mice often have smelly pee, so be careful where you keep them.

Getting ready

It's time to choose a home for your mice or rats. The bigger, the better! Get a large cage with different levels, things to climb, and places to hide. Don't forget toys and material to build nests and dig burrows.

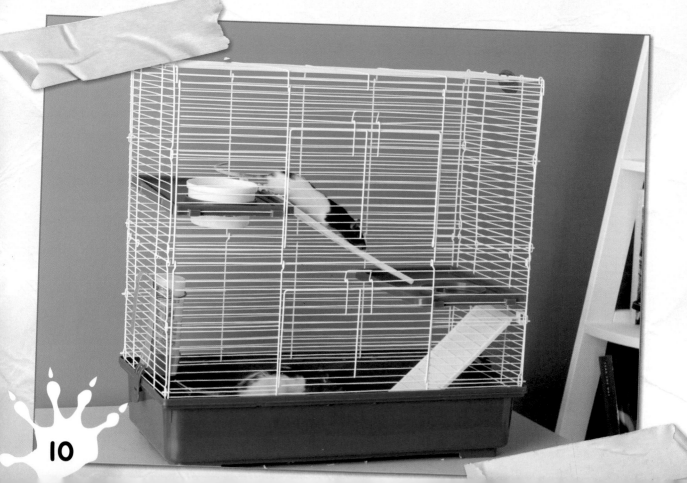

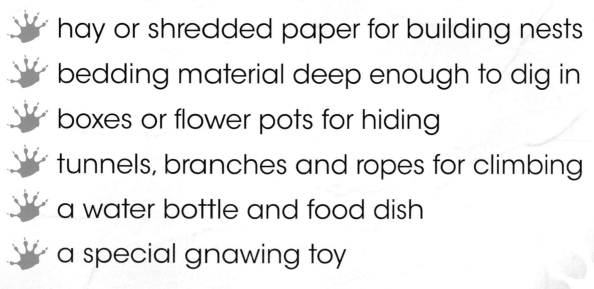

Squeak's shopping list:

- a large wire cage (for rats) or **vivarium** (for mice)
- hay or shredded paper for building nests
- bedding material deep enough to dig in
- boxes or flower pots for hiding
- tunnels, branches and ropes for climbing
- a water bottle and food dish
- a special gnawing toy

Welcome home

Moving to a new home can be scary.
Mice or rats will look for a dark place to hide
until we feel brave enough to start exploring.
Watch us carefully to make sure we don't fight.

Help us to settle in by finding the perfect place for our cage. Choose somewhere away from bright lights, **draughts** and loud noises. Mice and rats rest and sleep during the day, so make sure we won't be disturbed.

How to pick us up

Early morning and evening are the best times to handle rats and mice. We'll be awake and ready to play. Follow my tips to make sure your pets love being held.

Do not disturb

- Wash your hands before and after handling me.
- Talk to me and feed me treats to show you are friendly.
- Gently scoop me up with cupped hands.
- If I poo, pee or try to escape, it might mean I'm frightened. Put me back and try later.
- Never pick me up by my tail.
- Sit on the floor so I don't get hurt if I jump out of your hands.

Playtime

Mice and rats love exploring. Fill our home with tunnels, ropes, ladders and ramps for climbing. Get a special rat or mouse exercise wheel. Scatter food around my cage so I can play hide-and-seek.

When I'm used to being handled, let me play outside my cage. This is my chance to run, jump and explore a new area. Make sure there are safe hiding places. Keep dangerous things out of reach in case I nibble them.

Feeding time

Special mouse or rat food contains everything we need to stay healthy. Give us fresh pellets or cubes every morning and evening, so we always have food to eat. Make sure we always have fresh water, too.

Mice or rats like to nibble fresh fruit. Give us a few small pieces so we don't eat too much or too often. Some human foods make delicious treats, but others can make us very ill. Check out my tips on page 29.

Clean and healthy

Rats and mice are very clean animals.
We spend lots of time **grooming** ourselves.
Some of us like a bowl of shallow water to dip
our faces and paws. Sometimes we fill it with
food or bedding though. We're all different!

Like all rodents, I have front teeth that never stop growing. Ask your pet shop for special toys or wooden blocks that your mice or rats can **gnaw**. This will stop their teeth from growing too long.

Cleaning my home

I clean myself, but I can't clean my cage.
Clear away old food, droppings and damp
bedding every day. Sometimes I pee in one
place in my cage, so please clean here a lot!
Wash your hands after touching my toys – I
pee on things to make them smell like home!

Clean out the whole cage every week. Do it in the morning or evening when I'm already awake. Remember to wash my water bottle and toys. Leave some old nesting material behind so my cage still smells like home.

Visiting the vet

Most pet mice and rats live for two or three years. Take us to the vet every birthday for a check-up. The vet will make sure we're happy and healthy. They will check that our teeth are growing properly.

I can't tell you if I'm feeling unwell. Check me every day when we play and when you clean out my cage. Look for anything that is different from usual. Take me to the vet right away if you think I'm sick or injured.

No change, please!

Groups of rats or mice like to stay together for life. Please don't split me up from my friends, or put new pets in my cage. We might start fighting. If your rats or mice start fighting, make sure they have enough space, food, toys and hiding places.

If you go away, please ask someone to visit your house every day to look after us. Tell them how to clean our cage and feed us. They can let us out to play, but be careful they don't lose us! We'll look forward to seeing you again though!

Rat and mouse facts

- Rats and mice can hear sounds that you can't hear. They even "speak" to each other using squeaks that are too high-pitched for your ears.

- Big, open spaces make rats and mice feel scared. They always like to be near a safe hiding place.

- Rats and mice love to burrow and build nests. The nests help them to keep warm.

- Rats and mice can squeeze through very small holes. A young mouse can fit through a hole the size of a pencil!

Squeak's top tips

- Check my water bottle daily to make sure I haven't blocked it with my bedding.

- I love eating seeds, grains, and oats. Too many seeds or grains will make us unhealthy. Feed us oats sometimes instead!

- Some human foods make great treats, too. Try bread, cooked pasta and breakfast cereals.

- Never give rats and mice grapes, raisins, corn, citrus fruits, onions, chocolate, sticky foods, rhubarb, walnuts, lettuce or food made for other pets.

- Try to avoid travelling with us. If you do, make sure never to leave us in a hot car for a long time.

Glossary

animal shelter organization that cares for animals that do not have homes

breeder person who helps animals to have babies in an organized way

coat fur or hair that covers an animal

draught cool breeze inside a building from an open door or window

gnaw bite or chew something again and again

groom clean an animal's fur or skin

rescue centre organization that rescues animals that are lost, injured, or not being taken care of properly

rodent type of animal with front teeth that never stop growing, like rats and mice

vet person trained to care for sick and injured animals

vivarium tank with glass or plastic walls used as a home for fish or other small pets

Find out more

Books

Humphrey's World of Pets by Betty G. Birney
  (Puffin Books, 2013)

Pets Plus: Rats and Mice by Sally Morgan
  (Franklin Watts, 2011)

Websites

www.pdsa.org.uk/pet-health-advice/mice
www.pdsa.org.uk/pet-health-advice/rats
The PDSA website has advice about caring for pet rats and mice.

www.rspca.org.uk/allaboutanimals/pets/rodents/mice
www.rspca.org.uk/allaboutanimals/pets/rodents/rats
The website of the RSPCA (Royal Society for the Prevention of Cruelty to Animals) has information about pet rats and mice and how to look after them.

Index